The Children's Response

OTHER TITLES OF INTEREST

THE ACTION REPORTER
Armando Riverol

COMMUNICATION-STARTERS
Judy W-B Olsen

DRAWING OUT
Sharron Bassano and Mary Ann Christison

ENGLISH THROUGH DRAMA
John M. Dennis & Associates, Inc.

ENGLISH THROUGH POETRY
Mary Ann Christison

THE NATURAL APPROACH
Stephen D. Krashen and Tracy D. Terrell

LIVE ACTION ENGLISH (and Cassette)
Elizabeth Romijn and Contee Seely

LOOK WHO'S TALKING! Second Edition
Mary Ann Christison and Sharron Bassano

SOUNDS EASY (series)
Sharron Bassano

WORD WAYS CUBES
Bryan Benson and Lydia Stack

WORD WAYS GAMEBOARDS
Bryan Benson and Lydia Stack

WORD WAYS GAME CARDS
Bryan Benson and Lydia Stack

The Children's Response
TPR and Beyond toward Writing

Caroline Linse
Lower Kuskokwim School District
Bethel, Alaska

Illustrations by Kathy Barbour

Alemany Press
a division of
Janus Book Publishers, Inc.
Hayward, California

ISBN 0-88084-110-9

ed in the United States of America

7 8 9 0 1 2 3 4 D – P 0 9 8 7 6 5 4

JUL 0 4 2002

Contents

Foreword

There are few instructional materials for any subject, anywhere with which learners truly delight in using. The sixty lessons in *The Children's Response* are among these precious few.

This delight is one significant reason this book is particularly effective. The delight comes from the carefully chosen and deftly designed content and from the physical involvement of children and teacher. Physical involvement in learning is, unquestionably, fuller involvement. Movement, together with speech, is obviously a significant part of normal first language acquisition in children. The Total Physical Response approach is based on this fact and on two others—that there is a period in first language aquisition during which there is comprehension without speech and that all early and much of later acquisition is based on direct experience. This book uses all three of these important facts to great advantage to promote second *and* first language acquisition in the elementary classroom.

The Children's Response is the first book written specifically for use with children which is made up almost entirely of series of actions. Series, as François Gouin pointed out some one hundred years ago, help learners to remember due to the interrelation of the various actions.

Caroline Linse has written a wonderfully delightful book which is extremely effective. We are fortunate to have it.

Contee Seely
Elizabeth Romijn
Berkeley, California
January, 1983

Introduction

Basic Guidelines

The grammatical points found in these lessons are the same grammatical points presented in many American and British English as a Second Language programs for children. These lessons have been designed to supplement what is being presented in the basal ESL curriculum. A limited number of vocabulary items are introduced in each lesson. A maximum of one idiom is introduced per lesson.

The lessons are a pleasant way to introduce new grammatical patterns and items that young children and second language learners traditionally have trouble with. One cannot see a negative statement as clearly as it can be illustrated through sequences of actions.

Whenever I am introducing, or working on, a new grammatical point, I begin with a TPR lesson. After I feel that the students are comfortable with the lesson, I work on that particular structure in isolation through games and drills. I have found that children are more likely to use the new concept in their everyday communication if it has first been presented in a TPR lesson. It also helps to set out the props used in the TPR lessons in a place where children can work with them independently: this encourages peer teaching.

The Children's Response is based on James J. Asher's Total Physical Response method. Professor Asher has been doing research with the Total Physical Response method of language teaching for over twenty-four years. He has obtained dramatic results with all ages of language learners. TPR takes into account that people learn best when they are actively involved in the lesson—and understand the language they hear. This is especially true of children who developmentally have shorter attention spans and need to wiggle. Professor Asher is a psychologist at San Jose State University and has published a most valuable resource titled **Learning Another Language Through Actions: The Complete Teacher's Guidebook.** If you are working with older children, you may wish to use **Live Action English** by Elizabeth Romijn and Contee Seely.

In **The Children's Response,** each grammatical concept is presented twice. Both presentations emphasize or illustrate the same key grammatical concept. Either or both of the lessons may be used, but it is best to use only one lesson at a time. The first of these paired presentations requires no preparation and the simplest of materials: paper, pencil, chalk or crayons. Once you feel comfortable with the basic technique, these lessons can be considered as emergency, last minute, "I was out late last night" lessons. The second lessons require slightly more preparation and in some instances you may need to bring items from home.

How you use **The Children's Response** will depend on a number of factors, including the students' age, level of English background and willingness to participate in a group setting. Young children generally find the lessons fun. And when young children are shy about speaking, they sometimes become less inhibited about talking after pantomiming or carrying out the action sequences. Older children are sometimes reluctant to participate in a lesson at first, but their reluctance melts away and is often replaced with an eagerness to do more TPR lessons.

Children with a very limited command of English can enjoy these lessons and respond beautifully if not pushed too hard. The first five steps of each lesson can be used with an entire class of young children from non-English speakers to native English speakers. With older children, you may use the entire lesson with non-English speakers.

Young native English speakers can benefit from these lessons in a variety of ways. They can be the basis for language experience stories. They can be a way to teach creative writing: students can write their own sequences for each other to act out. Or you can use them as a method of teaching and checking the following directions and sequencing skills.

Children in grades K-6 can benefit from the presentations that follow. They can be used successfully with native English speakers and second language learners at all levels of English development in grades K-3. In the intermediate levels (4-6), they are most beneficial if used with ESL students at the beginning and the advanced levels.

How much oral communication you want the children to do will depend entirely on the group and the individual children. Some children do not respond orally at first. Others mouth the words voluntarily when a sequence is being repeated a second or a third time. I usually begin by asking them to just say key words such as *walk,* or *soap,* etc.

It's all right to exaggerate and be dramatic. Don't be afraid to do the absurd. Children enjoy and remember ridiculousness. Children adore playing teacher and these lessons capitalize on their enjoyment. The first few times, follow the procedures as listed for your particular teaching situation and then be creative. You may wish to use costumes, have the children write a story or even have them draw pictures to serve as prompting cues.

Most importantly, let these lessons be a way of enjoying teaching and enhancing the language of children from a wide variety of linguistic and cultural backgrounds.

K-3: BILINGUAL CLASSROOM

Prior to lesson introduce pertinent vocabulary with second language learners.

NATIVE SPEAKERS AND SECOND LANGUAGE LEARNERS

1. SETTING UP - Have students sit in a circle or other informal arrangement. Set up the situation in front of students. For some of the lessons you'll just need to grab a piece of chalk. For others you may need to bring items from home. Talk about what you'll be doing. "I am getting ready to draw a picture," etc.

2. DEMONSTRATION - Read the lesson while you or a native English speaker does the action.

3. (REINFORCEMENT) - Read the lesson while a native English speaker does the action.

4. ESL STUDENT MODELING - Read the lesson while a second language learner does the action.

5. TOTAL CLASS PARTICIPATION - Read the lesson and have the entire class carry out or pretend to carry out the instructions.

SECOND LANGUAGE LEARNERS

- Repeat step number 5.
- Change lesson sequence.
- Review vocabulary.
- Exaggerate lesson with pantomime.
- Use drills and games to reinforce grammatical concept.
- Create own sequences.
- Have students play teacher.

NATIVE SPEAKERS

- Change lesson sequence.
- Have students play teacher.
- Use as basis for language experience story.
- Record sequence of lesson with students.
- Create own sequences.

ESL Students

Before the lesson, spend time introducing pertinent vocabulary items.

Grades K-6
Divide students according to age.

1. SETTING UP - Have students sit in a circle or other informal arrangement. Set up the situation in front of students. For some of the lessons you'll just need to grab a piece of chalk. For others you may need to bring items from home. Talk about what you'll be doing, "I'm getting ready to draw a picture." etc.

2. DEMONSTRATION - Read the lesson while you do the action.

3. STUDENT MODELING - Read the lesson while a student does the actions.

4. REINFORCEMENT - Repeat step number 3.

5. TOTAL CLASS PARTICIPATION - Read the lesson and have the entire class carry out or pretend to carry out the instructions.

6. VARIATION - Change the lesson sequence.

Grades K-3

- Review vocabulary.
- Exaggerate lesson with pantomime.
- Play with props.
- Use drills and games to reinforce grammatical concept.
- Create own sequence.

Grades 4-6

- Have a student play teacher.
- Do pictograph or written word record of sequence.
- Ask more advanced students to do sequence with less advanced or beginning students.
- Exaggerate lesson with pantomime.
- Use drills and games to reinforce grammatical concept.
- Create own sequence. (Can be used in LEA if students are ready for written language work.)

CREATING LANGUAGE EXPERIENCE STORIES

After doing some of the presentations, you may wish to select some to use as a basis for Language Experience stories. Children should have some background in English and, if they are second language learners, they should have a written knowledge of their primary language. This approach is very successful with first and second language learners because it is child-centered and ensures oral language exposure in context prior to the written presentation. Thus the children's reading comprehension is also increased.

1. Choose a sequence from the book or **adapt** a group experience such as a cooking activity, science activity or a field trip. For example, the class could peel and eat a banana and then describe the activities. This would be an adaptation of **Eating Grapes** (page 2).

2. Have the students act out the sequence.

3. While the sequence is being performed, or as soon as possible afterwards, have students tell you what they are doing or what has been done. Act as a secretary and write down **exactly** what the children say. As a group, have children edit the story. *This is a very exciting stage.*

4. Read the story together.

5. Students may copy and illustrate the story, using pictures and stick figures in place of some of the nouns.

6. Display the stories in a prominent place in the classroom. Some of the stories may be run off on dittos and sent home with the children as a class newspaper.

INDEX OF GRAMMATICAL CONCEPTS

References

Asher, James J. *Learning Another Language Through Actions: The Complete Teacher's Guidebook* (Second Edition.) ©1982 Los Gatos: Sky Oaks

Krashen, Stephen D. and Tracy D. Terrell. *The Natural Approach: Language Acquisition in the Classroom.* © 1983 Hayward   : Alemany

Romijn, Elizabeth and Contee Seely. *Live Action English for Foreign Students.* ©1979 Hayward   : Alemany

Stevick, Earl W. *A Way and Ways.* ©1980 Rowley: Newbury

Specifically for use with children

Charles, C.M. *Teacher's Petit Piaget* ©1974 Menlo Park: Fearon

Cox, B.G. and J. Macaulay and M. Ramirez *Young Children Learning: Handbook for Teachers* ©1982. Elmsford: Pergamon.

CONCEPT: Imperative Commands
EXAMPLE OF: hop, run, walk
MATERIALS: none

Hop, Run, Walk

1. Hop.
2. Walk.
3. Run.
4. Jump.
5. Sit down and rest.
6. Get up.
7. Hop.
8. Walk.
* 9. Run.
10. Walk.
11. Jump.
12. Sit down and rest.

*If doing this indoors, your next command might be "Stop"

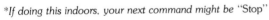

CONCEPT: Imperative Commands
EXAMPLE OF: eat, chew, swallow
MATERIALS: seedless grapes

Eating Grapes

1. Look at the grapes.
2. Turn on the water.
3. Put the grapes under the water.
4. Wash the grapes.
5. Don't use soap.
6. Shake the grapes dry.
7. Pick a grape.
8. Give it to a friend.
9. Pick another grape.
10. Chew it.
11. Chew it some more.
12. Swallow it.

Strawberries and raisins are also good to use.

CONCEPT: Commands
EXAMPLE OF: laugh, talk, run, cry
MATERIALS: none

Laugh or Cry

1. You're tired.
2. Rest.
3. You're sad.
4. Cry.
5. You're angry.
6. Run.
7. You're happy.
8. Laugh.
9. You have a story to tell.
10. Talk.
11. You're tired.
12. Rest.

CONCEPT: Commands
EXAMPLE OF: cover, make, put
MATERIALS: seeds, dirt, planting
containers, cup of water

Plant a Seed

1. Make a hole in the dirt.
2. Pick up the seed.
3. Put it in the hole.
4. Cover the seed with dirt.
5. Make another hole.
6. Pick up another seed.
7. Cover the seed with dirt.
8. Pick up the cup.
9. Pour a little water on the dirt.
10. Don't pour too much!
11. Put it on a shelf.
12. Come back and look tomorrow.

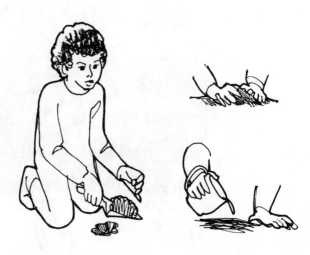

CONCEPT: Pronouns and Present
Continuous
EXAMPLE OF: I'm/you're walking/
running/drawing
MATERIALS: a piece of chalk

The Picture

1. I will draw a picture.
2. I'm picking up the chalk.
3. I'm drawing a circle.
4. I'm drawing two eyes.
5. I'm drawing a nose.
6. I'm drawing a mouth.
7. I'm drawing you.
8. You're smiling.
9. You're happy.
10. Now, you're frowning.
(Change smile to frown.)
11. You're sad.

CONCEPT: Pronouns and Present Continuous

EXAMPLE OF: I'm/you're walking/ running/drawing

MATERIALS: a pair of paper wings for child to use

A Flying Bird

1. You're a bird.
2. You're going to fly.
3. You're walking.
4. You're running.
5. You're running faster.
6. You're flapping your wings.
7. You're flapping *and* running.
8. WOW!
9. You're flying.
10. You're flying faster.
11. You're flying slower.
12. You're tired.
13. Good, you're resting.

CONCEPT: Definite Articles
EXAMPLE OF: This is *the* book.
MATERIALS: a book.

Read the Book

1. Go to the bookshelf.
2. Look at the books.
3. Pick up a book.
4. Look at the book.
5. Open the book.
6. Read the book.
   (Look at pictures and turn pages.)
7. Close the book.
8. Put the book away.

CONCEPT: Definite Articles
EXAMPLE OF: Cross *the* street.
MATERIALS: none*

Cross the Street

1. Walk to the curb.
2. Look up the street.
3. Look down the street.
4. A car is coming.
5. The car stopped.
6. Look up the street.
7. Look down the street.
8. No cars are coming.
9. Cross the street.
10. VERY GOOD!

*It is nice to do this as a mini-field-trip.

CONCEPT: Connectives
EXAMPLE OF: and
MATERIALS: none

Listen

1. Listen.
2. Jump and hop.
3. Hop and clap.
4. Clap and run.
5. Run and sing.
6. Sing and sit down.
7. Clap and rest.
8. Get up and walk.
9. Walk and clap.
10. Run and sing.
11. Sit and rest.

CONCEPT: Connectives
EXAMPLE OF: and
MATERIALS: *pictures of; a cat, fish, dog and bird

Pick the Animals Up

1. Look at the cat and the dog.
2. Pick up the cat and the dog.
3. Put the cat and the dog down.
4. Pick up the fish and the cat.
5. Don't let the cat get near the fish.
6. Put the cat and the fish down.
7. Pick up the fish and the bird.
8. Put the fish down.
9. Pick up the cat.
10. Look at the cat and the bird.
11. Don't let the cat eat the bird!
12. Put the bird and the cat down.
13. Oh, that's better.

*The pictures on pages 63-66 may be reproduced.

CONCEPT: Demonstrative Pronouns
EXAMPLE OF: this/that
MATERIALS: *a piece of paper taped to
the chalkboard and
crayons

A Pretty Picture

1. This is a crayon.
2. That is a piece of paper.
3. I will draw on that paper.
4. I'm drawing a tree.
5. That is a tree.
6. I will draw a sun with this crayon.
7. This is a sun.
8. That is a sun.
9. I'm drawing a flower.
10. That is a flower.
11. That is a picture.
12. This is a pretty picture.

Show the difference between this *and* that *by moving away from the picture to illustrate the concept,* that.

*Also see pages 67-69.

CONCEPT: Demonstrative Pronouns
EXAMPLE OF: this/that
MATERIALS: a big shoe and a little shoe

My Shoes Don't Match

1. This is a shoe.
2. That is a shoe.
3. This is a big shoe.
4. That is a little shoe.
5. This shoe is not the same as that shoe.
6. This is a big shoe.
7. This is a big shoe.
7. That is a little shoe.
8. I can't wear this shoe with that shoe.
9. This is a little shoe.
10. That is a big shoe.

CONCEPT: Possessive Pronouns
EXAMPLE OF: my/your
MATERIALS: paper and a pencil

Your Name On Your Paper

1. My name is _____(name)_____ .
2. Your name is _____(name)_____ .
3. Pick up your paper.
4. Put your paper on your desk.
5. Pick up your pencil.
6. Write your name on your paper.
7. Put your pencil down.
8. Look at your name.
9. Pick up your paper.
10. Give me your paper.

CONCEPT: Possessive Pronouns
EXAMPLE OF: my/your
MATERIALS: a coat

My Coat?

1. This is my coat.
2. Oh, no my name is not on my coat.
3. My coat is green.
4. Your coat is green too.
5. My coat has four buttons.
6. Your coat has four buttons too.
7. Look in the pocket.
8. My paper was in my pocket.
9. It has my name on it.
10. This is my coat.
11. Where is your coat?

CONCEPT: Possessive Pronouns
EXAMPLE OF: *her* skirt
MATERIALS: a piece of chalk

Her

1. Pick up a piece of chalk.
2. Draw a girl.
3. Draw lots of hair.
4. Draw a line from the hair to the girl.
5. That's her hair.
6. Draw a shoe.
7. Draw a line from the girl to the shoe.
8. That's her shoe.
9. Draw a skirt.
10. Draw a line from the girl to the skirt.
11. That's her skirt.
12. Her name is LaRee.

CONCEPT: Possessives
EXAMPLE OF: *her* skirt
MATERIALS: popsicle sticks, glue, crayons, construction paper, scissors

LaRee

1. Draw a picture of a girl.
2. Her name is LaRee.
3. Color her skirt.
4. Color her hair.
5. Color her shoes.
6. Color her ears.
7. Color her eyes.
8. Color her face.
9. She likes bananas.
10. Draw a banana in her hand.
11. Color her blouse.
12. Color the rest of her.
13. Cut LaRee out.
14. Meet LaRee!

See page 70.

CONCEPT: Possessive Pronouns
EXAMPLE OF: *his* shoe
MATERIALS: a piece of chalk.

His

1. Pick up the chalk.
2. Draw a boy.
3. Draw a shoe.
4. Draw a line from the boy to the shoe.
5. That's his shoe.
6. Draw a shirt.
7. Draw a line from the boy to the shirt.
8. That's his shirt.
9. Draw a pencil.
10. Draw a line from the boy to the pencil.
11. That's his pencil.
12. That's his shirt.
13. His name is George.

CONCEPT: Possessives
EXAMPLE OF: *his* shirt
MATERIALS: popsicle sticks, glue, crayons, construction paper, scissors

George

1. Draw a picture of a boy.
2. His name is George.
3. Color his pants.
4. Color his shirt.
5. Color his hair.
6. Color his eyes.
7. Color his shoes.
8. He likes apples.
9. Draw an apple in his hand.
10. Color his face.
11. Color his hair.
12. Color the rest of him.
13. Cut George out.
14. Paste him to a stick.
15. Meet George!

See page 71.

CONCEPT: Countable Nouns
EXAMPLE OF: eyes, flowers
MATERIALS: a piece of paper taped to the chalkboard, crayons

A Monster

1. Make a monster.
2. Pick up the orange crayon.
3. Draw three eyes.
4. Put the orange crayon down.
5. Pick up the blue crayon.
6. Draw four mouths.
7. Put the blue crayon down.
8. Pick up the purple crayon.
9. Draw eight legs.
10. Put the purple crayon down.
11. Pick up the green crayon.
12. Draw three noses.
13. Look at the scary monster.

CONCEPT: Countable Nouns
EXAMPLE OF: legs, flowers
MATERIALS: flowers for making a lei, a threaded needle (paper flowers may also be used)

A Lei

1. Pick up a flower.
2. Pick up a needle.
3. Put the needle through the flower.
4. Pick up another flower.
5. Put the needle through the flower.
6. Count the flowers.
7. Pick up another flower.
8. Put the needle through the flower.
9. Count the flowers.
10. Pick up another flower.
11. Put the needle through the flower.
12. Smell the flowers.
13. Look at the lei!
14. Put it on.
15. Take it off.
16. Give it to your friend.

CONCEPT: Plural of Nouns
EXAMPLE OF: 2 boats
MATERIALS: a piece of chalk

Two Boats

1. Draw one boat.
2. Draw another boat.
3. Erase two boats.
4. Draw one flower.
5. Draw another flower.
6. Erase two flowers.
7. Draw a can.
8. Draw another can.
9. Draw another can.
10. Erase two cans.
11. Erase one can.

CONCEPT: Plural of Nouns
EXAMPLE OF: three cherries
MATERIALS: *a plate, pictures of: 2 hot dogs, 3 cherries, 3 French fries

Lunch

1. I'm hungry.
2. I want some lunch.
3. Pick up a hot dog.
4. Pick up another hot dog.
5. Put the hot dogs on the plate.
6. Pick up the cherries.
7. Put the cherries on the plate.
8. Pick up 2 French fries.
9. Put the French fries on the plate.
10. Pick up another French fry.
11. Put it on the plate.
12. That is a funny lunch!

*See page 72.

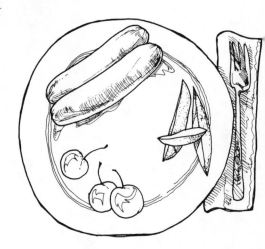

22

CONCEPT: Affirmative Responses
EXAMPLE OF: Yes, it is.
MATERIALS: a piece of chalk

Yes, It Is

1. Pick up the chalk.
2. Draw a picture of a girl in the class.
   (Look at the student you're drawing as you draw.)
3. Is that _(a girl, LaRee, Mary)_ ?
4. Yes, it is.
5. Put the chalk down.
6. Pick up the eraser.
7. Erase the girl.
8. Put the eraser down.
9. Pick up the chalk.
10. Draw a picture of a boy in the class.
11. Is that _(a boy, José, Tom)_ ?
12. Yes, it is.
13. Pick up the eraser.
14. Erase the boy.

CONCEPT: Affirmative Responses
EXAMPLE OF: Yes, it is.
MATERIALS: three or four postcards*

Look At It

1. Pick up a postcard.
2. Look at it.
3. Is it a ___(object in picture)___ ?
4. Yes, it is.
5. Put the postcard down.
6. Pick up another postcard.
7. Look at it.

8. Is it a _____ ?
9. Yes, it is.
10. Put the postcard down.
11. Pick up another postcard.
12. Look at it.
13. Is it a _____ ?
14. Yes, it is.
15. Put the postcard down.

*Try to choose postcards with one or two items on them.

24

CONCEPT: Negative Responses
EXAMPLE OF: No, it isn't.
MATERIALS: a piece of chalk

No, It Isn't!

1. Pick up the chalk.
2. Draw a picture of a boy in the class.
   (Look at the student you're drawing as you draw.)
3. Is that ___(student's name)___ ?
4. No, it isn't.
5. Put the chalk down.
6. Is that _____ ?
7. No, it isn't.
8. Pick up the eraser.
9. Erase the boy.
10. Put the eraser down.
11. Pick up the chalk.
12. Draw a picture of a girl in the class.
13. Is that _____ ?
14. No, it isn't.
15. Is that _____ ?
16. No, it isn't.

EXAMPLE OF: No, it isn't.
MATERIALS: chocolate syrup, a pitcher of milk, a glass

Chocolate Milk

1. Make some chocolate milk.
2. Pick up the pitcher of milk.
3. Pour some milk in a glass.
4. Is that chocolate milk?
5. No, it isn't.
6. Pick up the chocolate syrup.
7. Is that milk?
8. No, it isn't.
9. Pour the chocolate into the glass.
10. Is that plain milk?
11. No, it isn't.

26

CONCEPT: Negative Statements

EXAMPLE OF: Don't pick up the crayon.

MATERIALS: a piece of chalk, an eraser, a crayon

Rainy or Sunny

1. Pick up a piece of chalk.
2. Don't put it down.
3. Draw a tree.
4. Don't draw a house.
5. Don't draw a sun.
6. Draw rain.
7. Put the chalk down.
8. Don't pick it up.
9. Don't pick up the crayon.
10. Pick up the eraser.
11. Don't erase the flower.
12. Erase the rain.
13. Don't erase the tree.
14. Put the eraser down.
15. Don't pick up the crayon.
16. Pick up the chalk.
17. Don't draw rain.
18. Draw a sun.

CONCEPT: Negative Statements

EXAMPLE OF: Don't pick up the crayon.

MATERIALS: a plastic plate, a plastic cup, a plastic glass, a fork and a spoon

Don't Break It

1. Touch the glass.
2. Don't break it.
3. Pick up the plate.
4. Don't put it down.
5. Pick up the plate.
6. Put the plate down.
7. Don't break it.
8. Pick up the fork.
9. Put the glass down.
10. Don't put the fork down.
11. Don't pick up the glass.
12. Put the fork down.
13. Don't touch the fork.
14. Touch the spoon.
15. Pick up the cup.
16. Don't break it.
17. Pick up the fork.
18. Don't pick up the plate.
19. All right, pick it up.
20. But, don't break it.

CONCEPT: Interrogatives (questions)
EXAMPLE OF: What are you doing?
What's your name?
MATERIALS: none

What Are You Doing?

*1. What's your name?

2. Jump.

3. What are you doing?

4. Stop.

5. Walk.

6. What are you doing?

7. Hop.

8. What are you doing?

9. Stop.

10. Run.

11. What are you doing?

12. Stop and rest.

*This requires at least two people for all stages,
  including the initial demonstration.

CONCEPT: Interrogatives (questions)

EXAMPLE OF: What are you doing?
What's your name?

MATERIALS: a badge (can be made out of aluminum foil)

Lost

1. I'm a police officer.
2. Look at my badge.
3. You're lost.
4. What's your name?
5. How old are you?
6. Where do you live?
7. What's your mother's name?
8. What color is your house?
9. Are you hungry?
10. Are you thirsty?
11. I'll take you home.

CONCEPT: Regular Past Tense
EXAMPLE OF: I washed my nose.
MATERIALS: a piece of chalk

My Bath

1. Draw a moon on the board.
2. Last night I was very dirty.
3. Last night I took a bath.
4. I washed my toes.
   (Point to toes.)
5. I washed my feet.
6. I washed my ears.
7. I washed my nose.
8. I washed my fingers.
9. I washed my hands.
10. I washed my back.
11. It was hard to wash my back.
12. Now I am clean.

CONCEPT: Regular Past Tense

EXAMPLE OF: I washed my hands.

MATERIALS: a picture of; house, phone, bed, light, toothbrush, TV, book, a piece of chalk

Last Night

1. Draw a moon on the board.
2. Last night I walked home.
3. I talked on the phone.
4. I watched TV.
5. I brushed my teeth.
6. I crawled into bed.
7. I couldn't sleep.
8. I turned the light on.
9. I read a book.
10. I turned the light off.
11. I went to sleep.

CONCEPT: Adjectives
EXAMPLE OF: big, little, brown
MATERIALS: pencils, crayons, paper

Fruit Basket

1. Draw a brown basket.
2. Draw a green apple.
3. Draw a yellow banana.
4. Draw an orange orange.
5. Draw a red apple.
6. Draw a yellow lemon.
7. Draw a red cherry.
8. Draw a little grape.
9. Smell the fruit.
10. Look at the fruit basket.

CONCEPT: Adjectives
EXAMPLE OF: big, little, brown
MATERIALS: a big bag, a little bag, a big red book

Big and Little

1. Look at the little bag.
2. Look at the red book.
3. Pick up the little bag.
4. Pick up the red book.
5. Put the red book in the little bag.
6. It doesn't fit.
7. Put the little bag down.
8. Pick up the big bag.
9. Put the book in the big bag.
10. Put the bag down.
11. Oh, good it fits.

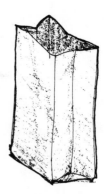

CONCEPT: Irregular Plural Form

EXAMPLE OF: one piece of,
two pieces of

MATERIALS: one piece of paper

Torn Paper

1. Pick up a piece of paper.
2. Tear it in half.
3. Put one of the pieces of paper down.
4. Tear the other piece of paper in half.
5. Put both pieces of paper down.
6. Tear the other piece in half.
7. Put both pieces of paper down.
8. Count the pieces of paper.
9. Write your name on each piece of paper.
10. Pick up one of the pieces of paper.
11. Tear it in half.
12. Put both pieces of paper down.
13. Write your name on the pieces of paper.
14. Count all of the pieces of paper.

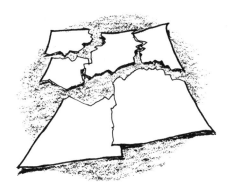

CONCEPT: Irregular Plural Form

EXAMPLE OF: one piece of
two pieces of

MATERIALS: a picture drawn on a piece
of paper, scissors

A Puzzle

1. Pick up the piece of paper.
2. Cut the piece of paper in half.
3. Cut the piece of paper in half.
4. Put one of the pieces of paper down.
5. Cut the other piece in half.
6. Put one of the pieces down.
7. Cut the other piece in half.
8. Put both pieces down.
9. Turn the pieces over.
10. Write your name on each piece.
11. Turn the pieces over again.
12. Mix them up.
13. WOW! You just made a puzzle.
14. Put the puzzle back together again.

CONCEPT: Irregularity of the verb to be
EXAMPLE OF: is/are
MATERIALS: a piece of paper taped to the chalkboard, crayons

Balls

1. Pick up a red crayon.
2. Draw a ball.
3. This ball is red.
4. Draw another ball.
5. These balls are red.
6. Put the red crayon down.
7. Pick up a green crayon.
8. Draw a ball.
9. This ball is green.
10. Draw another ball.
11. Put the green crayon down.
12. These balls are green.
13. Those balls are red.
14. I can't bounce those balls.

CONCEPT: Irregularity of the verb to be
EXAMPLE OF: is/are
MATERIALS: 3 cows ⎫ made out of
2 dogs ⎬ construction paper
2 pigs ⎭ with tape on the
back of each

The Farm

In front of students draw a picture of: a pig pen, dog house and barn on the chalkboard.

1. Pick up the animals.
2. Put a dog in the dog house.
3. A dog is in the dog house.
4. Put the other dog in the dog house.
5. The dogs are in the dog house.
6. Put the cows in the barn.
7. The cows are in the barn.
8. Put a pig in the pig pen.
9. A pig is in the pig pen.
10. The other pig is lonely.
11. Put the other pig in the pig pen.
12. The pigs are in the pig pen.
13. The animals are happy!

CONCEPT: Shapes (Specific Vocabulary Items)

EXAMPLE OF: circle, square, triangle

MATERIALS: a piece of paper taped to the chalkboard, crayons

An Ice Cream Cone and a House

1. Pick up a yellow crayon.
2. Draw a circle.
3. Put the yellow crayon down.
4. Pick up a brown crayon.
5. Draw a triangle under the circle.
6. Look at the ice cream cone.
7. Pick up a black crayon.
8. Draw a big square.
9. Draw a triangle on top of the square.
10. Draw a square window inside the big square
11. Draw another square window.
12. Draw another square window.
13. Draw another square window.
14. Put the black crayon down.
15. Pick up a brown crayon.
16. Draw a door.
17. Put the brown crayon down.
18. Look at the ice cream cone.
19. Pick up a crayon.
20. Put some ice cream in the ice cream cone.
21. THAT'S BETTER!

CONCEPT: Shapes (Specific Vocabulary Items)

EXAMPLE OF: circle, square, triangle

MATERIALS: crayons, scissors, paper prepared like the one below

A Paper Hat

1. Find the circle.
2. Pick up the red crayon.
3. Trace the circle.
4. Put the crayon down.
5. Find the triangle.
6. Pick up the blue crayon.
7. Trace the triangle.
8. Put the crayon down.
9. Pick up the scissors.
10. Cut out the circle.
11. Cut out the triangle.
12. Put the scissors down.
13. Put both edges of the triangle together.
14. Staple the edges.
15. Put on your hat.
16. You look gorgeous!

CONCEPT: Colors (Specific Vocabulary Items)

EXAMPLE OF: red, blue, green, brown, yellow, black, orange, purple

MATERIALS: crayons and a piece of paper taped to the board

Balloons

1. Draw a red circle.
2. Make it a red balloon.
3. Draw a blue circle.
4. Make it a blue balloon.
5. Draw a green balloon.
6. Draw a brown balloon.
7. Draw a yellow circle.
8. Make it a yellow balloon.
9. Draw a black balloon.
10. Draw an orange circle.
11. Make it an orange balloon.
12. Draw a purple balloon.
13. Draw a purple circle.
14. Make it a purple balloon.
15. Draw another red balloon.
16. Look at all the balloons.
17. Count them.
18. How many are there? (10)

CONCEPT: Colors (Specific Vocabulary Items)

EXAMPLE OF: red, blue, green, brown, yellow, black, orange, purple

MATERIALS: watercolors, paintbrush, a glass and a pitcher of water

Color Mixing

1. Pick up the pitcher.
2. Pour some water in the glass.
3. Put the pitcher down.
4. Put the paintbrush in the water.
5. Put the paintbrush in the yellow paint.
6. Put the paintbrush back in the water.
7. Stir it.
8. Watch it turn yellow.
9. Put the paintbrush in the blue paint.
10. Put it back in the water.
11. Stir it.
12. Watch the water turn green.

NOTE: *This exercise may be repeated with blue and red to make purple or with yellow and red to make orange. Food coloring may also be used instead of watercolors.*

CONCEPT: Numbers (Specific Vocabulary Items) 1-12

EXAMPLE OF: one, two, three . . .

MATERIALS: a piece of chalk

Lots of Apples

*1. Pick up the chalk.

2. Draw lots of apples.

3. Draw some more apples.

**4. Close your eyes.

5. Open your eyes.

6. Oh, no! Seven apples are missing!

7. Draw nine more apples.

8. Close your eyes.

9. Open your eyes.

10. Oh, no! TEN APPLES ARE MISSING!

11. Draw eleven more apples.

12. Don't close your eyes!

*This demonstration requires at least two people for the initial modeling stages.

**When the apples "disappear" erase them very lightly from the board.

CONCEPT: Numbers (Specific Vocabulary Items) 1-12

EXAMPLE OF: one, two, three . . .

MATERIALS: dice, a piece of chalk

The Dice Game

1. Pick up the dice.
2. Throw the dice.
3. What did you get?
4. Pick up the chalk.
5. Write the number on the board.
6. Put the chalk down.
7. Pick up the dice.
8. Throw the dice.
9. What did you get?
10. Are you sure?
11. Count it again.
12. Pick up the chalk.
13. Write the number on the board.
14. Put the chalk down.
15. Ask a friend to play with you.

CONCEPT: Prepositions
EXAMPLE OF: in
MATERIALS: a piece of paper taped to the chalkboard, crayons

Fish in a Fish Bowl

1. Pick up a black crayon.
2. Draw a fish bowl.
3. Put the crayon down.
4. Pick up a green crayon.
5. Draw a fish in the fish bowl.
6. Put the green crayon down.
7. The green fish is in the fish bowl.
8. Pick up an orange crayon.
9. Draw a fish in the fish bowl.
10. Draw another fish in the fish bowl.
11. Put the orange crayon down.
12. The orange fish are in the fish bowl.
13. Pick up a purple crayon.
14. Draw a fish in the fish bowl.
15. Put the purple crayon down.
16. Draw some water in the fish bowl.
17. A purple fish is in the fish bowl.
18. The fish like the water.

CONCEPT: Prepositions
EXAMPLE OF: in
MATERIALS: a toy rabbit and a hat

In the Hat

1. Look at the hat.
2. Don't let anyone see.
3. Nothing is in the hat.
4. Have everyone close their eyes.
5. Hide the rabbit in the hat.
6. Is the rabbit in the hat?
7. Look in the hat.
8. Is the rabbit in the hat?
9. Look again.
10. Put your hand in the hat.
11. Here it is.
12. The rabbit was in the hat.

CONCEPT: Prepositions
EXAMPLE OF: on
MATERIALS: a piece of paper taped to the chalkboard (the paper should be horizontal), crayons

The Placemat

1. Pick up a crayon.
2. Draw a cup on the placemat.
3. Draw a plate on the placemat.
4. The plate is on the placemat.
5. The cup is on the placemat.
6. Draw a fork on the placemat.
7. Draw some cake on the plate.
8. The fork is on the placemat.
9. The cake is on the plate.
10. Draw some flowers on the placemat.
11. Enjoy the cake!

Children may wish to use placemat for a special occasion.

CONCEPT: Prepositions
EXAMPLE OF: on
MATERIALS: a cup, plate, fork, knife and spoon

Setting the Table

1. Pick up the cup.
2. Put it on the table.
3. The cup is on the table.
4. Pick up the plate.
5. Put it on the table.
6. The plate is on the table.
7. Pick up the fork.
8. Put it on the table.
9. The fork is on the table.
10. Pick up the knife.
11. Put it on the table.
12. The knife is on the table.
13. Pick up the spoon.
14. Put it on the table.
15. The spoon is on the table.
16. The table is set.

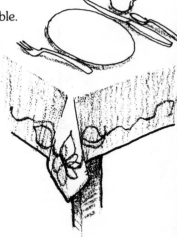

CONCEPT: Prepositions
EXAMPLE OF: under
MATERIALS: a table, chair, book, pencil,
piece of paper

Under the Table or Chair

1. Pick up the book.
2. Put it under the table.
3. Pick up the pencil.
4. Put it under the table.
5. Pick up the book.
6. Put it under the chair.
7. Pick up the piece of paper.
8. Put it under the chair.
9. Pick up the piece of paper.
10. Put it under the table.
11. Put it under the chair.
12. The piece of paper is under the chair.
13. Pick up the crayon.
14. Put it under the piece of paper.

CONCEPT: Prepositions
EXAMPLE OF: under
MATERIALS: (Prior to lesson make a tree, big bird, little bird, 4 eggs, nest, sun and cat out of construction paper)

The Bird

1. Tape a tree to the chalkboard.
2. Tape a big bird under the tree.
3. The bird is under the tree.
4. Tape an egg under the bird.
5. Tape another egg under the bird.
6. Tape another two eggs under the bird.
7. There are four eggs under the bird.
8. Tape a nest under the eggs.
9. The nest is under the eggs.
10. Tape a sun to the chalkboard.
11. Tape a cat under the nest.
12. The cat is looking up at the nest.
13. Tape some grass under the cat.

Children enjoy talking about the cause and effect relationship between the cat, eggs and bird

CONCEPT: Prepositions
EXAMPLE OF: over
MATERIALS: a pencil, a piece of chalk, a chair, a book

Over

1. Put the pencil, chalk and book on the floor.
2. Step over the pencil.
3. Step over the chalk.
4. Pick up the pencil.
5. Hold the pencil over the chair.
6. Put the pencil down.
7. Step over the chair.
8. Step over the book.
9. Pick up the book.
10. Hold the book over the chair.
11. Pick up the pencil and the chalk.

CONCEPT: Prepositions
EXAMPLE OF: over
MATERIALS: a rope

The Rope Game

1. Pick up the rope.
2. Put the rope on the floor.
3. Step over the rope.
4. Pick two helpers.
5. Each helper holds an end of the rope.
6. Step over the rope.
7. Helpers, lift the rope a little.
8. Step over the rope.
9. Helpers, lift the rope a little.
10. Step over the rope.
11. Step over the rope.

CONCEPT: Prepositions
EXAMPLE OF: up, down
MATERIALS: a piece of chalk

Arrows

1. Stand up.
2. Look up.
3. Pick up a piece of chalk.
4. Draw an arrow going up.
5. Draw an arrow going down.
6. Look down.
7. Draw an arrow going up.
8. Draw an arrow going down.
9. Draw an arrow going down.
10. Put the chalk down.
11. Look up.
12. Sit down.

CONCEPT: Prepositions
EXAMPLE OF: up, down
MATERIALS: none

Climbing

*1. You're going to climb up a tree.
2. Look at the tree.
3. It's a tall tree.
4. Lift up one foot.
5. Lift up the other foot.
6. Climb up.
7. Climb up.
8. Climb down.
9. Climb down.
10. Put one foot down.
11. Put the other foot down.
12. Sit down and rest.

This is especially successful if done outside next to a big tall tree.

CONCEPT: Prepositions
EXAMPLE OF: off
MATERIALS: none

Funny Positions

1. Put your foot on your knee.
2. Take your foot off your knee.
3. Put your foot on your chin.
4. Put your hand on your back.
5. Take your hand off your back.
6. Take your foot off your chin.
7. Put your chin on your hand.
8. Take your chin off your hand.
9. Put your chin on your knee.
10. Take your chin off your knee.
11. Pretend to put a hat on.
12. Pretend to put a ring on.
13. Pretend to take the hat off.
14. Pretend to take the ring off.

CONCEPT: Prepositions
EXAMPLE OF: off
MATERIALS: 2 magnets, a nail, a steel paperclip, an eraser, a button

Two Magnets

1. Pick up the nail.
2. Put the nail on the magnet.
3. It sticks to the magnet.
4. Take the nail off the magnet.
5. Put the nail down.
6. Pick up the eraser.
7. Put the eraser on the magnet.
8. Push the eraser off the magnet.
9. Pick up the paperclip.
10. Put it on the magnet.
11. Take the paperclip off the magnet.
12. Put the paperclip down.
13. Pick up the other magnet.
14. Put both magnets together.
15. Pick up the paperclip.
16. Put it on the magnets.
17. Take the magnets apart.

CONCEPT: Prepositions
EXAMPLE OF: at
MATERIALS: pencil, paper book

Look At It

1. Look at the boy.
2. Look at the paper.
3. Look at the book.
4. Look at the teacher.
5. Look at the pencil.
6. Look at the girl.
7. Look at the paper.
8. _____(Student's name)_____ , pick up the paper.
9. Look at the girl with the paper.

CONCEPT: Prepositions
EXAMPLE OF: at
MATERIALS: 10 flash cards, 2 of each;
blank, circle, face, man,
monster (arranged in order
listed below)

The Monster Comes and Goes

1. Look at the card.
2. Look at the circle.
3. Look at the face.
4. Look at the man.
5. Look at the monster.
6. Look at the monster.
7. Look at the man.
8. Look at the face.
9. Look at the circle.
10. Look at the card.
11. The monster is gone.

CONCEPT: Prepositions
EXAMPLE OF: through
MATERIALS: paper strips, glue

Paper Chains

1. Pick up a paper strip.
2. Put some glue on one end.
3. Glue both ends together.
4. Pick up another strip.
5. Put some glue on one end.
6. Put the strip through the circle.
7. Glue both ends together.
8. Pick up another strip.
9. Put some glue on one end.
10. Put the strip through the circle.
11. Glue both ends together.
12. Pick up another strip.
13. Put some glue on one end.
14. Put the strip through the circle.
15. Glue both ends together.
16. That's a pretty paper chain.

CONCEPT: Prepositions
EXAMPLE OF: through
MATERIALS: a picture of: a boy, bear, bee, lion, mother, house

Through the Roof

1. My brother came through the door.
2. A bear came through the door too.
3. A bee came through the window.
4. A lion came through the door.
5. A big bird came through the window.
6. The bear didn't like the lion.
7. The bear went through the door.
8. The bear broke the door.
9. The bird didn't like the lion.
10. The bird went through the window.
11. The lion was sad.
12. My mother was mad.
13. The lion went through the window.
14. The lion broke the window.
15. My mother went through the roof.

Manipulatives for this exercise can be made very easily. Children enjoy making their own house, animals and people.

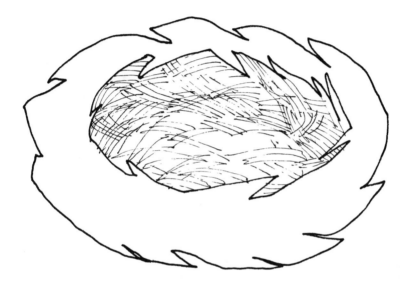

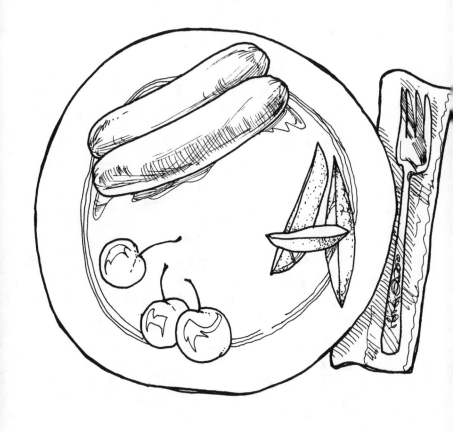